SMALL GAME
HUNTING

JUDY MONROE PETERSON

rosen publishing's
**rosen
central**

New York

To Dave, for his continued support and kind heart

Published in 2011 by The Rosen Publishing Group, Inc.
29 East 21st Street, New York, NY 10010

Library of Congress Cataloging-in-Publication Data

Peterson, Judy Monroe.
Small game hunting / Judy Monroe Peterson. — 1st ed.
        p. cm. — (Hunting: pursuing wild game!)
Includes bibliographical references and index.
ISBN 978-1-4488-1242-4 (library binding) —
ISBN 978-1-4488-2272-0 (pbk.) —
ISBN 978-1-4488-2279-9 (6-pack)
1. Small game hunting—Juvenile literature. 2. Fowling—Juvenile literature. I. Title.
SK340.P48 2011
799.2'5—dc22

                                                                    2010009841

Manufactured in the United States of America

CPSIA Compliance Information: Batch #W11YA: For further information, contact Rosen Publishing, New York, New York, at 1-800-237-9932.

On the cover: Small game hunters look for squirrels in trees. Squirrel hunting season usually opens in late summer and lasts until February.

CONTENTS

The most frequently hunted animals in the United States and Canada are small game. The small game hunted most commonly include rabbits, squirrels, woodcocks, and quail. Small wildlife hunting is popular in North America because it offers many opportunities for hunts that are readily available and do not cost much money. Hunters often have easy access to these wild animals. Sometimes they need to go only a few miles to get into small game habitats. Rabbits and squirrels are found in every state and much of Canada. Woodcock hunting occurs during the fall when the birds migrate from the northern states and Canada to southern locations. Quail live in the prairies, fields, and marshlands of many states. Woodcocks and quail are called upland birds.

People can make frequent, short trips to hunt small wildlife. The trips do not require much advance planning or expensive equipment. Finding and shooting these small targets is challenging and exciting. Small animals are fast, cautious, and well adapted to their environment. Small game hunters usually feel a sense of satisfaction and accomplishment when using their skills. When they are successful, they harvest low-fat, delicious meat.

Hunting is a tradition for many people. Family or friends often enjoy the outdoors by hunting small game with beginning hunters. Lifelong friendships frequently develop between hunting partners.

Hunting small game is a great way to get into nature and watch wildlife close up. Many people experience a sense of well-being after spending time in the woods, fields, or marshes. Small game hunting is good mental and physical exercise. Hunters often walk long distances in an animal's habitat.

Although hunting small game is not easy, it is a great choice for beginning hunters. Typically, they can hunt small game all day, after the sun is up and until the sun goes down. They can hunt squirrels and rabbits during many months of each year. The season for woodcock and quail hunting is usually several months every fall. Often two or three partners hunt small game together year after year. In many families, hunting is an annual tradition. The older members teach hunting skills to the young people. Other individuals hunt for the sport of the chase. They may have their animals mounted and displayed in their homes or hunting cabins.

The management and conservation of wildlife is largely dependent on licensed hunters. Construction of highways, houses, and farmland is steadily destroying the habitats of small game. By buying licenses and paying special taxes on hunting equipment, hunters provide money to the states to enforce hunting laws, manage wildlife, and maintain conservation programs.

Small game is owned by the public. State and federal laws control hunting to avoid the overharvest and extinction of wild animals. The laws are changed to allow an increased game harvest if a population grows beyond its available food and shelter. To manage their wildlife populations, states have hunting seasons for each type of wild game. People can legally hunt an animal only during its hunting season. All states have bag limits for each small game animal hunted. The number of harvested game animals in a bag limit may change annually as a wildlife management tool. In addition to knowing the laws, hunters must also learn how to use their weapons, prepare for a hunt, and have knowledge about small wildlife.

CHAPTER I

LEARNING TO HUNT

*H*unting small game in the fields and woods and understanding their habits and habitats require both skill and knowledge. To be a successful hunter takes time, practice, and training. Good hunters must know how to accurately and safely use their weapons. Squirrels and rabbits are often hunted with rifles, shotguns, smooth bore muzzleloaders, and archery. The shotgun is the most common type of firearm used to hunt quail and woodcocks. Using the correct weapon can make a hunt more enjoyable and increase the chance of success.

The purchase of hunting firearms is controlled by federal and state regulations. A hunter must be of legal age to buy a firearm for hunting. If a hunter is underage, an adult must buy and register the gun. Every state regulates the hunting season for each type of animal. The government also authorizes what firearms and archery can be used

Successful small game hunting requires practice to learn precise shooting skills before the actual hunt. Scopes like the one shown here magnify the target, which helps the hunter to shoot accurately.

for hunting. States require beginning hunters to pass a hunter training course before they can buy a license.

Rifles

A common firearm used to shoot wild rabbits and squirrels is the .22 rifle. Many hunters choose this firearm because shots taken for small game are often within 50 feet (15 meters). A .22 rifle has little or no recoil (kickback). Youthful hunters should use a small-caliber rifle that fits the length of their arm.

Many small game hunters have a scope attached to the top of their rifle. To aim quickly, hunters line up the crosshairs (guides) inside the scope. Hunters can see an animal better because of the magnification of the scope. Scopes with lower power work best for close-range shooting of small game. A typical scope used for small game is one-and-a-half times (1.5 X) magnification. This means that an animal appears one-and-a-half times closer to the hunter. Small game hunting can also be successfully accomplished without a scope.

Hunters can select or use different bullets to find what works best when hunting small game. Different powered bullets are available for the .22 rifle, including shorts, longs, and long rifles. Small game hunters can effectively use any of these cartridges. The most popular small game bullet is the .22 caliber long rifle. Hunters can find the caliber of a rifle stamped on its barrel. Some small game hunters prefer a combination gun with a .22 caliber barrel on top and a 20-gauge shotgun barrel on the bottom.

Various rifle models with different actions are available. The most popular model for hunting small game is a bolt action, in which the bolt is operated by hand. Other rifle actions used are pump, break, semiautomatic, and lever. Hunters often choose an action depending on where and what small animal they will hunt.

Shotguns and Muzzleloaders

The shotgun is the only firearm used to hunt quail and woodcocks because after about 400 feet (122 meters), the lead or steel shot loses power quickly and drops to the ground harmlessly. The shot is powerful at close range and spreads out in a pattern effective up to 100 feet (30 m). The expanding shot pattern provides multiple chances to harvest quail and woodcocks. Any gauge shotgun can be used for small game. Many small game hunters prefer to use light loads with small lead shot because they increase the number of pellets that are aimed at the target.

Shooting with a Bow and Arrow

To hunt small game with a bow and arrow is difficult, but rewarding. Compared to hunters using firearms, bowhunters must get closer to small wildlife to shoot accurately. The reason is simple: arrows do not travel as far as bullets. Shooting a bow and arrow is more difficult than shooting a firearm. Archers need to build up their shooting muscles and be able to concentrate and judge distances accurately. To successfully bowhunt, archers learn how to stand correctly and how to position their body and hands. An important skill for bowhunters is the precise placement of an arrow. Small, fast-moving animals present few chances to aim accurately. Key to being a good archer is the ability to relax and not to force the arrow toward a target. This means that archers must wait for a sitting, stationary target. For safety, hunters should always inspect their bowstring before a hunt and replace frayed strings.

Shotguns are available in five common gauges: .410 bore, 16-gauge, 20-gauge, 12-gauge, and 10-gauge. Although upland game birds are hunted with all gauges, the 12-gauge shotgun is the most popular. Beginning hunters might start with a .410 bore, 16-gauge, or 20-gauge to minimize the recoil. Actions for shotguns are the break open, bolt, pump, double barrel, and semiautomatic. Many quail and woodcock hunters prefer the 20-gauge double barrel or automatic for fast aiming and shooting.

Muzzleloaders that have smooth bores and are loaded with lead or steel shot are categorized as shotguns and can legally be used to

Using a compound bow allows the hunter to pull back the string and wait for a perfect shot. Bowhunters practice on targets to build up their arm and shoulder muscles.

hunt rabbits, squirrels, woodcocks, and quail in many areas. Hunting upland birds with muzzleloaders loaded with lead shot is challenging because a hunter can take only one shot with this type of gun. The reload requires one to two minutes. By then, the birds have flown out of shooting range.

Archery

Many hunters use archery when they begin hunting small game. Although any bow can be used to hunt squirrels and rabbits, many hunters prefer the compound bow. They can draw the arrow back and hold it while they wait for an animal to come into shooting range. They can do this because a compound bow reduces the amount of force needed to hold a bow that is ready for release. Bows are rated in pounds to pull the string back. For example, a bow rated at 30 pounds (14 kilograms) requires 30 pounds (14 km) of force (strength) to pull back the string to draw an arrow. Bows in the area of 20 to 30 pounds (9 to 14 km) work well for harvesting small animals.

The blunt point arrow is preferred when hunting squirrels and rabbits. The arrow tip flairs, forming a wide striking surface. For squirrel hunting, blunt points are used with flu-flu arrows. Flu-flu is a type of arrow for short distance shooting. The feathers on flu-flu arrows are large. By using the blunt and flu-flu, bowhunters can shoot accurately up to 50 feet (15 meters). If an arrow misses the target, it falls harmlessly to the ground.

Using Weapons Safely

States offer a youth hunter education program. This training program requires beginning hunters to know and demonstrate safe weapon handling and shooting. During the course, beginning hunters learn to

Expert shooters provide valuable instruction on the proper techniques of shooting, such as breath control and eye-finger coordination. These skills help a hunter to accurately place a bullet on a distant or moving target.

treat every firearm as if it is loaded. They are taught to keep the gun unloaded until they are actually hunting. When carrying a gun while hunting, beginners learn to keep their fingers away from the trigger and leave the safety switch on. The safety switch is a mechanical action that can fail, so hunters learn never to assume it is on. Firearms can shoot accidently if the trigger pulls against brush or if the weapon falls to the ground.

When handling a gun, beginners are taught never to fire at only sound or movement or where hunters or other people might be.

This young man is shooting clay pigeons. Shooting under the guidance of an expert on a practice range can greatly improve a hunter's ability to shoot upland birds. All shooters are required to wear eye and ear protection.

Although .22 caliber is small, bullets can travel up to 1 mile (1.6 kilometers). When shooting, hunters must always know what is behind the target. They should never shoot animals at the top of a hill or in a tree without a backstop because of the danger to people or property beyond the target. For their own protection, hunters need to wear ear protectors and shooting glasses. Beginning hunters learn to store firearms and bullets in secure and separate places when not hunting or target shooting. Books and hunter training sites on the Web provide more information on safe hunting.

Safety is the highest priority for every hunter. Some hunters learn safety skills from family or friends who teach younger hunters. Other beginning hunters attend hunter education courses that are government sponsored. Local shooting or conservation clubs teach classes in archery and gun shooting and safety hunting skills. These hunter education courses cover small game identification, hunting regulations, and firearm and archery shooting and safe use.

Hunters have an ethical duty to shoot accurately and not wound a targeted small animal. Good hunters practice at shooting ranges to become skilled in the use of their gun or archery equipment. Some specialized shooting ranges have indoor and outdoor moving targets. Beginning hunters need to practice at targets placed at close ranges. They should practice shooting at longer ranges as their skills improve.

Shotguns require training and practice to follow a target and shoot at the right moment to hit a flying bird. To practice for shooting upland birds, the three main types of shotgun shooting at targets are skeet shooting, trapshooting, and sporting clays. Skeet shooting is shooting at clay pigeons (disks) that are flung into the air at high speed from different angles. In trap shooting, people shoot at clay pigeons that are thrown away from them in five different positions. Sporting clays is more difficult than trap or skeet because the targets are thrown at many different distances, angles, speeds, and heights. All three shotgun shooting methods are great ways to practice shooting in preparation for a quality hunt. Woodcock hunters tend to focus on skeet shooting for practice.

CHAPTER 2

RESPONSIBILITIES OF HUNTERS

All small game hunters have laws to follow and are personally responsible for their actions. Every state has rules that provide for the safety of other people, the controlled harvest of wildlife, and respect for private property. Each hunter has a duty to protect the land, water, and wildlife resources.

Learn the Laws

The harvest of small game animals is regulated by federal and state laws. Hunters must know and follow these rules. For example, hunters must buy a license to hunt squirrels, rabbits, quail, or woodcocks. They must know what type of gun or archery equipment can be used during each small game season. Regulations describe the number and type of small game. States set the months and days when each type of small game can be hunted legally.

Game wardens enforce hunting laws, including the safe use of guns. They can inspect hunters and their equipment for compliance with all hunting laws at any time.

States have bag limits for small game based on the available population for that animal. While in the field, hunters cannot have in their possession more than the daily bag limit for the target animal. Game wardens can stop hunters and ask to see how many small game animals are in their daily possession limit.

All states require that hunters have their hunting license and personal identification in their possession while hunting. This rule allows the positive identification of hunters if requested by law enforcement officials. Small game hunters renew their license every year, which is only valid for the season. All states have a detailed description of their hunting laws available in free booklets or on each state department of natural resources' Web site.

Hunting Ethics

Ethical hunters behave according to what is right. Ethics are personal decisions beyond what federal or state laws require. When a hunter is fair and polite to other hunters, other people, and personal property, good ethics is the result. Proper behavior while someone is hunting is a personal code. This set of behaviorial standards is termed the "hunter's code," and it is as important as hunting regulations.

Here is an example of ethical behavior when hunting upland birds. When dogs point at hiding birds, beginning hunters or hunters who have not taken any game can move to the most likely flushing zones. This action increases their chance for a successful shot. Sometimes ethical behavior might involve two people who want to hunt the same area for small game. Instead of arguing, they might decide to share the location or alternate the days that each hunter is at that spot. Poachers are unethical people who hunt illegally. They might

Smart small game hunters always wear blaze orange clothing and accessories so that other hunters can see them. This very bright orange color is also called safety orange.

break small game laws by going over their bag limit or hunt without a license and harvest small game. They might harvest wildlife outside of its season or during the season without following the regulations. When caught, poachers are fined and lose their hunting privileges. Hunting weapons and vehicles are often seized and not returned.

Accessing Land

Small game animals live in the wild without boundaries. However, hunters must know where it is legal to hunt them. They need to avoid trespassing on private property, which means they always need to know their location. Hunting without permission on private land that has a "No Trespassing" or "No Hunting" posting is a crime.

Migratory Bird Harvest Information Program

Every season, people who hunt woodcocks and other migratory game birds are required to be licensed with the Migratory Bird Harvest Information Program (HIP). The U.S. Fish and Wildlife Service and state wildlife agencies jointly run this program. The purpose of HIP is to increase the accuracy of harvest estimates of migratory birds. This information is used to help wildlife managers make decisions concerning hunting seasons, bag limits, and population management. People who buy a license to hunt migratory birds in states are also required to buy a HIP permit. The permit might be a card, stamp, or other item, and it must be renewed each year. The procedures to sign up for HIP vary from state to state. Hunters must carry proof of their HIP license with them when hunting migratory birds.

Landowners need to be approached for permission to hunt on their land. Private land with farm animals, equipment, and farmland must be treated carefully by hunters. On completion of the hunt, it is appropriate for hunters to say a genuine "thank you" to the landowner. If the hunt is successful, many hunters share their game with the landowners. In repayment for the privilege of hunting on private land, hunters will often help the landowner with a special project. Farmers, for example, might need labor during certain seasons of farming, such as putting up hay, building fences, or helping with the harvest. Most landowners will allow helpful and respectful hunters to return for additional hunts.

The government owns public land, including national forests and state wildlife management areas. Hunting on public property for small game requires hunters to treat the land and public campgrounds with respect. For instance, hunters should clear and carry away their own and other litter in the area during their hunt.

Positive Image

Many people enjoy being outdoors and watching wildlife. Responsible hunters make certain that their actions are not offensive. Some non-hunters are afraid of hunting firearms or develop antihunting opinions based on the behavior of irresponsible hunters. Hunters carrying guns and archery equipment should show a positive image and use common sense and courtesy. To be respectful, hunters in public settings should store unloaded guns in cases and out of sight when they are not in use.

Hunters who do not take unfair advantage of small game animals are practicing "fair chase." An example of an unfair chase is if a person in a vehicle drives, herds, or takes any rabbits or upland birds from a moving vehicle or boat under motor power. Responsible hunters know their guns or archery equipment, how it functions, and how to not wound their target. If an animal is wounded, hunters should try to track and recover it. Responsible hunters often help each other during recovery. For a hunter to become an accurate shot and not wound an animal requires that hunter to have lots of target practice.

After small game is harvested, hunters have a duty to use the meat. They can share the meat with nonhunters. Successful hunters often photograph or preserve their harvested animals. As hunters travel to and from hunting areas, they should cover or put their harvested animals in coolers so that they do not offend nonhunters.

Hunters always need to practice safety. Until they are ready to shoot, they keep their guns unloaded with open actions—and the safety on. The gun muzzle is pointed downrange or in a safe direction.

Safety

A hunting gun and bow are dangerous because of the power of bullets or arrows. Safety must be on the mind of every hunter at all times. Hunters need to be alert for and responsible to other people, including other hunters in the area. Every hunter needs to obey the laws regulating hunting and respect the hunting area of others. The "zone of fire" is a term used for an area around a hunter where shooting can be done safely. When they are hunting alone, people can shoot in any direction at their small game target if they have a safe backstop to stop the bullet in the event that they miss.

Group hunting for small game such as rabbits and upland birds is fun and can be productive. However, it is important that the hunting partners always know the location of each other. Partners need to establish a zone of fire before they begin their hunt. Planning a group hunt increases hunting success and protects the safety of each partner. Sometimes, more than one hunter may harvest the same rabbit, woodcock, or other small game. When several hunters are responsible for the harvest, a decision must be made as to who takes possession of the animal. Group hunters may share equally in the number of animals harvested, or they may decide that the youngest hunter receives the prized animal.

Working Together to Support Wildlife

Wildlife conservation programs sponsored by the government guarantee a healthy wildlife population. Sometimes, a particular wildlife population declines and could become extinct. When this happens, the animal is endangered and cannot be hunted by law. As cities, road systems, and farmland become larger, the natural habitat of animals is often destroyed. As a result, the populations of small game animals may decrease. Hunting clubs and associations work with non-hunting organizations to encourage a healthy wildlife population. Together they buy large areas of wild land where small game can live and thrive. Responsible hunters support healthy wildlife populations by following the legal hunting season and harvesting only the allowable number of animals.

Nonhunters and hunters must continue to work together to guarantee stable wildlife populations for future generations. For example, rabbit populations often boom every nine to eleven years. If they get too large, the animals cannot find enough food. They might eat most or all of certain plants in an area. Without enough food, the rabbit populations will starve. They might get sick and infect other wild animals with disease. Hunters help in these situations by thinning or reducing small animals like rabbits, thus keeping them from overpopulating an area.

CHAPTER 3

BEFORE A HUNTING TRIP

Small game hunting is a great way to become acquainted with the natural world and the outdoors. Hunters need to do some planning before a hunting trip, starting with finding a place to hunt. This place could be as close as their backyard or a clump of nearby trees. Sometimes, people have to search for a hunting spot. Studying small animals in their environment is a good idea before actually hunting. This knowledge, combined with shooting and outdoor skills, will help small game hunters be successful.

Finding a Hunting Spot

Finding a place to hunt is an important step in planning. Wildlife managers and conservation officers can tell hunters where to get any necessary reservations and permits. These officials sometimes know farmers

Hunters constantly need to know their location in the field or woods so that they can safely return to their starting point. A global positioning system (GPS) or a compass is an important tool to have while hunting.

or ranchers who would like hunters to reduce the numbers of rabbits or squirrels on their land. Beginners can ask more experienced hunters or members of a hunting group for suggestions. If a good hunting spot is on private property, hunters can check the Web sites of the office of the local assessor or county to find the owner. Public land, such as national forests, is often open to hunting. Hunters should check with the U.S. Forest Service about hunting on federal land.

People must contact the landowner of private land and ask permission to hunt for a particular small game animal. To scout (look at) the area, hunters should contact the landowner before hunting season begins. Scouting helps hunters learn about an area and its wildlife. Topographic and aerial maps also provide information useful to someone unfamiliar with a particular area.

Animal Habitat and Behavior

To increase the chance of finding and shooting small animals, hunters need to understand the animals and

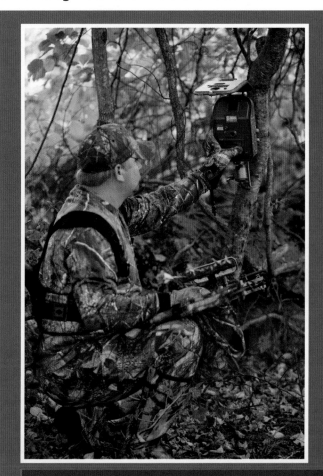

Scouting an area by walking or taking auto photos is a requirement for successful hunting. A camcorder like the one in this photograph is a useful device that can provide a hunter with additional information about game animals' habits.

Squirrels are found close to most hunters' homes and provide an inexpensive hunt. Many people often find the best time to hunt squirrels is soon after sunrise.

their habitats. Small game animals live where they have plant food and shelter. They do not travel far. However, woodcocks migrate great distances. When hunters find where wildlife feed or rest, their success of harvest increases. Small wild animals have keen senses of sight and hearing, which alert them to danger. Squirrels, rabbits, quail, and woodcocks react quickly by fleeing or hiding when hunters come too close.

Squirrels

Hunters usually harvest two types of squirrels for meat: gray squirrels and fox squirrels. Gray squirrels live in the eastern half of the United States and in several regions of the West, and in southern parts of Canada. They weigh about 1.5 pounds (680 grams) and are about 18 inches (46 centimeters) in length, which includes their big, bushy tail. Gray squirrels prefer hardwood trees (trees with broad leaves) or mixed forests with nut trees like oak, hickory, beech, pecan, and walnut. They live in tree holes, or build nests in trees. They are active year-round. Larger than gray squirrels, fox squirrels measure 19 to 30 inches (48 to 76 centimeters) long and weigh up to 3 pounds (1.4 kilograms). They inhabit the same eastern area of the United States as gray squirrels, but they range slightly more to the west. These prefer large hardwood trees, borders of cypress swamps, and thick grasses or bushes.

Squirrels are frisky and intelligent animals. They eat nuts, seeds, some fruits, insects, and bird eggs. They also like the buds and leaves of trees. In the fall, gray squirrels store away nuts and seeds for the winter. They place them in hollow logs, in holes in trees, or under leaves. They later find them by their keen sense of smell. Fox squirrels spend most of their waking time looking for nuts and other food.

Rabbits live in a small home range, equal to several city blocks. By following the tracks of a snowshoe rabbit in the snow, hunters have a good chance of finding it.

Rabbits

The most harvested types of rabbit in the United States are cottontail and snowshoe. Cottontails live across much of the United States except the Far West, and are they also found in areas of southern Canada. From nose to fluffy, white tail, they measure 14 to 19 inches (36 to 48 cm), and weigh 2 to 4 pounds (0.9 to 1.8 kg). They prefer to live in forests with open areas nearby, heavy brush, and tall grasses. They eat green plants. If food is in short supply, cottontails will chew the twigs and bark of trees and shrubs.

Using Dogs for Small Game Hunting

Hunting squirrels and rabbits with dogs can be effective with dogs that are well trained. Many types of dogs can be used to locate a squirrel and indicate its position by barking up a tree. Squirrel hunters use different kinds of dogs, such as bird hunting dogs, curs, feists, collies, rat terriers, and coonhounds. Hounds such as beagles or basset hounds are trained to follow the scent of game animals, including rabbits. Beagles are particularly popular for rabbit hunting because they are small and can get through brambles and brush.

Gundogs help hunters who use guns for birds such as quail and woodcocks. There are flushing dogs such as spaniels, pointing dogs such as setters, and retrievers. Pointers and setters point their body toward game that is hidden. Retrievers pick up birds that have been shot and bring them back to hunters. Flushing dogs flush, or chase, birds from brush and thick grass.

Although the snowshoe rabbit is really a hare, it is usually called a rabbit. Their winter-white fur changes to brown after the snow melts in the spring. Snowshoes live in most of the forests of the northern United States, Alaska, south along the Rocky and Appalachian mountains, and in much of Canada. They prefer thick brush underneath trees. They eat the bark of trees and shrubs and also twigs, grasses, and other plants. A little larger than cottontails, snowshoes are about 18 inches (46 cm) in length and weigh 3 to 4 pounds (1.4 to 1.8 kg). They also have taller hind legs and longer ears than cottontails. With their larger, furry feet, snowshoe rabbits move swiftly atop snow.

Quail

Five types of quail are usually hunted in the United States: bobwhite, California, Gambel's, scaled, and mountain. An important game bird, the Bobwhite lives year-round in most of the eastern half of the United States up to southern Minnesota and South Dakota, and in eastern Washington and Oregon. They eat mostly seeds of grass and weeds. They also feed on grains in farmlands, acorns, insects, and berries. They roost (sleep or rest) along wooded streams, the edges of woods, and wet and grassy areas. Bobwhites average about 10 inches (25 cm) in length and 8 ounces (227 grams) in weight. Fast runners, they seldom fly. If in danger, they will fly short distances up to 30 miles (48 kilometers) per hour.

The California quail's range is through the Pacific states, and the Gambel and scaled inhabit the American Southwest. All three birds prefer semiarid desert brush areas. Largest of all the quail, the mountain quail mostly occurs in the Pacific states. They live in higher locations with lots of oak trees and short grass. The Gambel, scaled, and mountain quail eat weed and brush seeds.

Different types of quail are found throughout much of the United States. This Gambel's quail is sitting on a tree branch in Phoenix, Arizona.

Woodcocks

Woodcock is the name of several types of birds that live in moist woods, near streams, lowland pasture regions with tall grass, and in sheltered wet areas. This land includes stands of alder, aspen, birch, and poplar along the banks of streams, beaver ponds, and marshes. Hunters focus on the American woodcock, which appears east of the Mississippi River and north to southern Canada. The woodcock is a migratory bird. Flying at night in short hops, woodcocks usually follow the same routes south and north each year. They winter from New Jersey to Missouri and

A woodcock is a small bird about the size of a person's fist. Its feathers are brown, black, and rust, with black bands across the top of the head.

south to the Gulf Coast, and then fly north in February or early March to nest and raise their chicks. Adult birds measure about 11 inches (28 cm) long and have a chunky body and short legs and wings. They use their long bill to probe the mud for earthworms and grubs (soft, thick, wormlike larvae of certain beetles). They also eat insects, weed seeds, and berries. Because their eyes are set far back on their head, they can easily see danger. The woodcock is mostly tan and brown. These earthy colors camouflage the bird in its habitat of wood and dead leaves and help protect it from enemies.

Planning Ahead

Sometimes, hunters walk long distances, so being in good physical condition is important for an enjoyable hunt. Hunters must be prepared for unexpected situations or emergencies when they are scouting or hunting. It is important that hunters always tell someone where they are going and when they expect to return. Outdoor skills are necessary for hunters to know—for example, how to build a fire and signal for help if that should become necessary.

Besides a basic survival kit, hunters often bring other items, including a small knife. Binoculars help them look for small game and identify legal small game animals. They carry a compass or use a global positioning system (GPS). Hunters may want to carry cell phones in case they have to make emergency calls. Many states require hunters to wear blaze orange clothing so that other hunters can see them. Even if not required by law to do so, hunters might wear blaze orange vests and hats. Many squirrel hunters also wear camouflage clothing, which helps keep animals from seeing them in the woods. It is a good idea for hunters to wear outdoor gear such as waterproof boots, brush pants, and a jacket that does not catch on burrs.

CHAPTER 4

WAYS TO HUNT

Small game hunters need to know multiple ways to help make their hunt effective. The method used for a particular hunt depends on many factors, such as the animal and land that is to be hunted, the number of people who are in the hunting group, the weather conditions, and the type of weapon that will be used. Hunters must also consider wind direction for quail and woodcocks, and how close they will be to buildings and non-hunting people. Small game will run or hide in a predictable way if an unusual scent, noise, or movements from a hunter occur.

Squirrels

Successful squirrel hunting depends on finding a stand of trees where they feed and rest. A stand of oak trees produces acorns, which are the favorite food of squirrels. If acorns are in short supply, they eat other

Some squirrel hunters like to move through the woods hunting their prey. Others prefer to find a comfortable spot to sit and wait for their prey to come to them.

kinds of nuts. Because squirrels blend in well with their surroundings, they may be difficult to see, especially if leaves are on the trees. Squirrels are also good at hiding and move quickly from tree to tree.

Squirrel hunting season typically opens in late summer and continues to February. Many states have a summer hunting season. Hunters search for squirrels in trees. Early in the season, the animals only go to the ground to pick up acorns and other seeds that have fallen. They spend more time on the ground to gather, dig, and store nuts later in the season. To find where squirrels feed, hunters look for piles of small pieces of chewed nuts and shells under trees. In light snow or mud, hunters can easily see where squirrels have been scratching through the snow or leaves to retrieve nuts and seeds.

Other Ways to Hunt Squirrels

Some people successfully hunt squirrels with a dog, which will search back and forth on the ground for the animals. Upon finding a squirrel, the barking dog chases it into a tree and then sits by the tree until the hunter arrives. The hunter usually finds the squirrel on the opposite side of the tree from the dog. Two other squirrel hunting methods can be productive. One is to team hunt with a partner. A squirrel typically hides on the opposite side of a tree trunk to get away from a hunter. By team hunting, a squirrel cannot hide on the other side of the tree without being seen by the hunters. Another method is to float hunt in canoes or flat-bottom boats along streams bordered by nut trees. Squirrels like to be close to water and will live in the nut trees, such as oak, that line the streams' banks.

The most common squirrel hunting method is to walk slowly through the woods on a day without much wind. Hunters listen for the sounds of leaves rustling and squirrels chattering to locate the animals. Squirrels are not sensitive to human odor, but they have excellent vision. They can detect movement far before hunters know squirrels are in the area. Once hunters find a good spot, they sit quietly against a tree and look for squirrels. Otherwise, they use a tool called a squirrel call to chatter back to the squirrel. The call and lack of movement soon relaxes the alerted squirrels. They will start feeding again, presenting excellent targets. Many times, several squirrels in an area can be called in over a short period of time. Sometimes, a hunter tosses a stick or rock on one side of the tree and then slips quickly to the other side. The motion frightens squirrels to the side of the hunter.

When squirrel hunting, archers use flu-flu arrows so that the arrow drops to the ground after 50 feet (15 m). Because .22 caliber bullets can travel 1 mile (1.61 km), squirrel hunters must have a backstop, which is usually a tree branch or trunk, or a hill behind a tree. If the hunter's shot misses an animal, the bullet will lodge harmlessly in a backstop. Shotgun and muzzleloader lead shot are very dangerous at close range, although after 500 feet (152 m) they represent little danger. Safe hunters must make sure that the shot at the target does not hit any livestock, people, or equipment behind it.

Rabbits

Most rabbit hunting is usually done with one or two people. Single hunters typically jump shoot rabbits. In this method, they slowly move through thick grass or brush and look for hiding places of rabbits, such as brush piles or windblown trees. Shelter belts also make excellent homes for small game animals, especially rabbits. These strips of trees and bushes are planted around farmland to reduce the erosion of the soil caused by heavy rain or wind. When hunters get close, the hidden rabbit jumps up, runs about 100 feet (30 m), and then stops. While the rabbit is running, hunters stand still at the hiding place. Once the rabbit stops, they pick up a viable target of the animal and make the harvest. A single hunter might use a dog to hunt. Then the hunter and dog slowly move through a rabbit's habitat. When a rabbit jumps out of its hiding place, the hunter sends the dog on the animal's track. The hunter stays where the rabbit was jumped. The rabbit runs quickly to escape as the dog chases it. A rabbit pushed hard by a dog will run a long distance. However, it runs in a large circle, usually back to where it was jumped. When the rabbit returns, the hunter can harvest it.

Rabbit hunting is also done in small groups. One person rattles on the hiding place with sticks or jumps on the hiding place, scaring the rabbit out so that the partner can harvest it. Another way is that one hunter might quickly walk after the moving rabbit, while the other hunter stays where the rabbit was jumped. A scared rabbit will run in a large circle and then will return to its home shelter, where the hunter may be able to shoot it.

Rabbit hunting is especially successful with a snow cover on the ground. Rabbits live and feed in a small area of about 5 acres (20,235 sq m). When hunters find rabbit tracks in the snow, they know the animals are close and hunting in that spot may be productive. Rabbits tend to run on their same game trail, making paths in the snow. Skillful hunters look for this type of rabbit trail in the snow and then hunt in the area. All methods of rabbit hunting lend themselves to the .22 rifle, small gauge shotguns, and bow and arrow. In many states, rabbit hunting season typically opens in late summer and continues until February or March.

Quail

Quail hunting season varies by state, but it is usually in the fall. Quail are regularly found in a covey (group) along brushy strips of land, such as fence lines, ditch lines, railroad tracks, or shelter belts. Hunters look for a circle of droppings to locate quail because they sleep back-to-back as a covey in a circle to conserve warmth and guard against predators. They tend to use the same spot for several nights. Individual hunters usually walk slowly toward the birds to flush a covey of quail. A group of two or three partners can be effective. The hunters fan out in a line

Hunting with a dog requires much practice in hunting together as a team. Many bird hunters find that their relationship with their dog is both challenging and rewarding.

and slowly walk through quail habitat, hoping to jump the birds and get multiple shots. Most hunters will shoot the birds as they flush, but refrain from chasing the singles, which allows the unharvested birds to regroup.

The only firearm used to hunt quail is the shotgun. The most common shotguns are the 12- and 20-gauge with lead or steel shot ranging from size 4 to 8. It is important that a hunter picks a single bird to shoot because shooting at a covey seldom brings down a bird. Quail are shot in the air. All kinds of dogs can be effective in hunting quail. Pointing dogs cover more ground and hold the birds until hunters can get into position to shoot. Retrievers, such as the springer spaniel, are better at flushing and retrieving wounded or harvested birds. Compared to pointers, flushers and retrievers work closer to the hunters. They may be more effective when birds are not holding (staying in their hiding place), as the hunters are more likely to be closer to the flush.

Woodcocks

Early fall is the time to hunt woodcocks. At that time, the birds are flying on their migratory routes, going from their northern home to their southern home. Hunters look for areas with moist or wet soil or shallow standing pools of water where migrating woodcocks like to feed. They also search for whitewash, or droppings, on the ground where the birds have been feeding. Woodcocks tend to come to feeding areas an hour before sunset.

A dog is needed to flush woodcocks because the birds hold very tight. Hunters can nearly walk on them before they flush. Different kinds of dogs can be effective when hunting woodcocks. Some hunters use pointers to flush the birds. Retriever dogs find wounded or harvested woodcocks.

When upland birds are shot, they may fall long distances from the hunter. The use of a retrieving dog is important to find the harvested birds.

Hunters shoot woodcocks as they rise or just before they level off into the air. Otherwise, the birds weave and dart in the air, making them a difficult target. When woodcocks are flushed, they fly about 50 to 75 yards (46 to 69 m) and then land. If flushed again, the birds repeat their flying and landing pattern. If hunters miss their target the first time, they can probably try to follow and shoot again. Many states allow only two to four woodcocks per day during the season.

CHAPTER 5

AFTER THE HARVEST

*A*fter harvesting small game, hunters need to retrieve the animal, then dress (remove the intestines and internal organs) it as soon as possible. Quickly processing a harvested animal helps ensure healthy, safe meat and good eating. After transporting the animal to camp or home, it is dressed (if not already finished) and kept cool until it is butchered (cut up into smaller pieces). The basic equipment needed to dress and butcher squirrels, rabbits, or upland birds is latex gloves, a sharp pocketknife, plastic bags that seal, and paper towels.

After the animal is dressed, it is left whole for roasting or cut into smaller pieces for cooking. People use a sharp knife or game shears (scissors) to cut up the meat. Next, hunters remove any pellets, shot, or BBs in the meat. After the meat is washed in cold water, it is ready to be cooked or frozen for later use. Plastic bags with locking

Many hunters take photographs after a successful hunt. Pictures are a great way to share with family and friends memories of hunts gone by. A quality hunting photograph can provide hunters with an opportunity to tell their hunting stories.

seals are an excellent way to safely freeze small game meat. Small game meat is delicious, lean, and can be cooked in many ways.

Processing Small Game

Some hunters skin their squirrels or rabbits to tan their hides. The hides can be used to trim gloves and other clothing. People might use or sell squirrel hides and tails for making artificial flies (trout fishing bait). Sometimes, they will take a hide to a taxidermist to be preserved and mounted for display. This professional starts by covering a premade foam model of the squirrel or rabbit with special glue. Then the tanned hide of the animal is carefully stretched and fitted on the model. Glass eyes are then glued into place. After the glue dries, the squirrel or rabbit is ready to be put on display in a special place in the home or cabin. Schools and science museums often have mounted animals for study.

Squirrels

Squirrels must be dressed and skinned after shooting. If the temperature is warm, the meat can begin to spoil quickly. Hunters often dress harvested squirrels in the field. To begin, they flip the animal onto its back. Using a sharp knife, they cut the underside of the tail and the tailbone. Then they cut around the squirrel's middle and step on the tail near the body. While the tail is held down, they pull the rear legs up, and peel the skin up and off. Next, the front legs are cut off, the skin is removed, and the head is cut off. Finally, the back legs are removed and the remaining skin is pulled off.

Next, hunters flip the squirrel over so that its belly is up. They carefully cut down the rib cage through the pelvic bone (front part of the hip bone). As they cut, hunters take care not to nick the stomach and intestines. Once the animal's back legs are spread open, the intestines

People often display mounted small game animals in recreation rooms and cabins. The three-dimensional animals preserve the special time of the hunt and provide a lifetime of memories.

and internal organs are pulled out, and the cavity of the animal is wiped clean with paper towels, leaves, or snow. Then the legs are cut off and placed into cold water. The ribs are cut off next and discarded as offal. Hunters typically cut the animal into five or six pieces: two front legs,

A game bag that hunters can carry like a backpack comes in handy for collecting carcasses of small game. Many backpacks come in blaze orange, which helps others see the hunter.

two back legs, and one or two back pieces. Then the butchered meat is washed in cold water and kept cool or frozen.

Rabbits

When the temperature is warm, it is critical to dress rabbits in the field to quickly cool the meat. Hunters field dress a rabbit by first putting the animal on its back. They slit the underside up to the neck and remove the intestines and internal organs. Then they clean the cavity with paper towels, leaves, or snow.

Skinning a rabbit can be done in the field or at camp or home. Hunters have different methods of skinning the animal. One way is to

Safety While Processing Small Game

People can get sick from processing rabbits infected with tularemia, a disease caused by the bacterium *Francisella tularensis*. The bacterium can enter through the butcher's skin, eyes, or mouth. To be safe, wise hunters wear latex gloves while dressing, skinning, or butchering the animals. The gloves can be found at the personal medical or pharmacy section of most general retail stores. Outdoor and hunting supply stores also carry them. While processing, people should not touch their mouth or eyes. When they are finished, many hunters put their gloves and discarded animal parts into plastic bags and seal them. Then they put the bags into the trash so that pet cats and dogs cannot reach them. Next, they wash their hands well, even if they wore latex gloves. To reduce the risk of spoilage, hunters immediately chill small game meat by putting it into a cooler with ice, refrigerator, or freezer.

pinch the hide up and away from the middle of the spine. Next, they cut the hide from the spine down the sides, being careful not to cut the meat. With both hands, they hold and pull the hide in opposite directions so that the legs are skinned up to the feet. Then hunters remove the feet, head, and tail.

To prepare rabbit for cooking, people usually cut the front legs from the body at the shoulder. After that, they cut and remove the hind legs at the hip. They separate the rib section from the loin and cut the back into two or three pieces, depending on the size of the animal. Because the rib cage does not have much meat, hunters remove it. They might use the rib cage and front legs to make soup.

Quail and Woodcocks

If the weather is warm, hunters often dress upland birds in the field soon after they are shot. In cool weather, many people wait until they are at their vehicle, camp, or home. If the birds are not field dressed, hunters put them into a cloth bag or a hunting vest with a large pocket on the back. Others clip the birds to their belt. Once home, they skin the bird or pluck the feathers. Some people leave the skin on to help keep the small birds moist during cooking. Next, the wings and neck are cut off at the body and discarded. The legs are snipped off just above the ankle joint. After the birds are cleaned under cold running water, they are patted dry and are now ready to cook or be packaged and frozen.

Cooking Small Game

The meat of small game is lean, meaning it has little fat. Squirrel meat is dark, and rabbit meat is white. The age of an animal affects the texture and taste, which in turn affects the cooking methods. Young squirrels and rabbits usually have tender meat, but older animals may have tougher meat. Bobwhite quail meat is a light color, and the average dressed weight is 6 ounces (170 g). A woodcock has both white and dark meat, with an average dressed weight of 5 ounces (142 g). Light meat is drier than dark meat and usually cooks faster.

People cook squirrels, rabbits, and small game birds in many ways, including roasting, grilling, broiling, baking, frying, or smoking. The meat is prepared in other healthy ways, such as in soups, stews, and casseroles. Cooking squirrels, rabbits, or game birds slowly in a Crock-Pot with vegetables and broth or another liquid provides a simple, but delicious meal.

Preparing for the Next Hunt

Before leaving the area, hunters should thank the other hunters and private land owners who helped in the successful harvest. It is a good idea to share small game meat with the landowner and with relatives or nonhunting friends. Even if the hunt did not produce results, the landowner should be thanked for the use of the private land.

Preparation for the next hunt begins as soon as hunters come home. They should clean, dry, and safely store their firearm or bow-hunting gear. It is a good idea to write in a journal the details of the last hunt. Special notes should be made that recall what parts of the hunt were successful or failed. The most important planning tool is to write down all the equipment and clothing that hunters used and keep this as a check-off list for the next hunt. Hunters' success at small game hunting increases as their skills improve. Small game hunters can apply these skills to other types of hunting, such as big game or varmint hunting. Small game hunters have many

Regular cleaning and proper storage are essential for the safe operation of hunting equipment. Responsible hunters check their firearms after the hunt and have a gunsmith occasionally inspect them for worn or broken parts.

opportunities to refine their hunting skills. They can sign up with a club to learn how to shoot expertly. They can join an outdoor off-season club to help with habitat or conservation projects. Members in other organizations can teach small game hunters other skills, such as how to use a GPS. To learn more about animal behavior, hunters can study at natural history museums or zoos. Books and magazines are available to help people learn more about guns, ammunition, hunting dogs, game calls, and archery equipment that can be used in future hunts. A great way to learn the sport of small game hunting is to help a friend become a good hunter.

ammunition Bullets and gunpowder used in firearms.

archery The skill of shooting with a bow and arrow; an archer's weapons.

bag limit The number of a particular type of animal that a hunter can harvest during a day.

barrel The metal tube of a rifle.

bore The inside diameter of a gun barrel.

butcher To process an animal's meat into usable sizes.

caliber The inside diameter of the barrel of a rifle or the diameter of a bullet.

camouflage Anything that conceals people or equipment by making them appear to be part of the natural surroundings.

conservation Protection and preservation of nature.

endangered Describing an animal population in such small numbers that it is in danger of becoming extinct.

extinct No longer existing.

dress To prepare a recently harvested animal so that its body temperature lowers and the meat stays fresh.

flush To cause a hidden bird to fly away suddenly.

game Wild animals hunted for food or sport.

global positioning system (GPS) Handheld computers that can calculate an exact position using a global positioning satellite.

habitat The area or environment where an animal lives.

harvest The act of shooting and recovering an animal.

illegal Against the law.

latex Thin rubber.

migrate To move from one location to another location every season.

muzzleloader A firearm that is loaded through the muzzle, which is the discharging end of the barrel.

offal The intestines, internal organs, and other body parts that are discarded after an animal is butchered.

poacher A person who takes game in a forbidden area or game that is illegal to take.

possession limit The maximum number of a type of animal that can be in a hunter's possession at any time.

safety A device on a firearm that keeps it from being fired.

scope A small telescope on a rifle barrel.

season The length of time to hunt specific game.

semiautomatic shotgun A kind of shotgun that can fire a shell after every trigger pull, without manually reloading.

target Something that is aimed at to shoot by firearms or bow and arrow.

taxidermist A professional who preserves and mounts the hide and head of an animal on a three-dimensional body form.

trespass To unlawfully enter a person's property.

upland game birds Birds that are hunted on land as opposed to over water.

Canadian Parks and Wilderness Society

506-250 City Centre Avenue

Ottawa, ON K1R 6K7

Canada

(800) 333-9453

Web site: http://www.cpaws.org

This organization focuses on protecting many important areas of Canada's
wilderness.

Canadian Shooting Sports Association

7 Director Court, Unit #106

Vaughan, ON L4L 4S5

Canada

(888) 873-4339

Web site: http://www.cdnshootingsports.org

The Canadian Shooting Sports Association promotes shooting sports, including hunting and archery. It supports and sponsors competitions, youth
programs, and conducts training classes.

International Hunter Education Association

2727 West 92nd Avenue, Suite 103

Federal Heights, CO 80260

(303) 430-7233

Web site: http://www.ihea.com

The International Hunter Education Association is the professional association
for state and provincial wildlife conservation agencies and the instructors
who teach hunter education in North America.

National Bowhunter Education Foundation

P.O. Box 180757

Fort Smith, AR 72918

(479) 649-9036

Web site: http://www.nbef.org

This organization provides bowhunting education and classes across the
United States.

National Rifle Association of America

11250 Waples Mill Road

Fairfax, VA 22030

(800) 672-3888

Web site: http://www.nra.org

The National Rifle Association of America provides firearms education
throughout the world.

National Shooting Sports Foundation

Flintlock Ridge Office Center

11 Mile Hill Road

Newtown, CT 06470-2359

(203) 426-1320

Web site: http://www.nssf.org

The mission of the National Shooting Sports Foundation is to promote,
protect, and preserve hunting and the shooting sports.

National Wildlife Federation

11100 Wildlife Center Drive

Reston, VA 20190-5362

(800) 822-9919

Web site: http://www.nwf.org

The National Wildlife Federation works to protect and restore wildlife habitat.

U.S. Fish and Wildlife Service

1849 C Street NW

Washington, DC 20240

(800) 344-9453

Web site: http://www.fws.gov

This government agency is dedicated to the conservation, protection, and enhancement of wildlife and plants and their habitats. Its primary responsibility is management of these important natural resources for the American public.

U.S. Forest Service

c/o Office of Communication

Mailstop: 1111

1400 Independence Avenue SW

Washington, DC 20250-1111

(800) 832-1355

Web site: http://www.fs.fed.us

An agency of the U.S. Department of Agriculture, the Forest Service manages the millions of acres of public lands in national forests and grasslands.

Web Sites

Due to the changing nature of Internet links, Rosen Publishing has developed an online list of Web sites related to the subject of this book. This site is updated regularly. Please use this link to access the list:

http://www.rosenlinks.com/hunt/sgh

Andrews, Harris, and James A. Smith. *The Pocket Field Dressing Guide: The Complete Guide to Dressing Game*. Accokeek, MD: Stoeger Publishing Company, 2007.

Fisher, Dave. *Rabbit Hunting: Secrets of a Master Cottontail Hunter*. Jupiter, FL: Creative Outdoors, 2004.

Gooch, Bob. *The Ultimate Guide to Squirrel Hunting: Everything You Need to Know to Hunt This Popular Game Animal*. Guilford, CT: Lyons Press, 2004.

Gross, W. H. *Young Beginner's Guide to Shooting & Archery: Tips for Gun and Bow*. Minnetonka, MN: Creative Publishing international, 2009.

Johnson, M. D. *Successful Small Game Hunting: Rediscovering Our Hunting Heritage*. Iola, WI: Krause Publications, 2003.

Kaufman, Ken. *Kaufman Field Guide to Birds of North America*. Boston, MA: Houghton Mifflin Harcourt, 2005.

Lauber, Lon E. *Bowhunter's Guide to Accurate Shooting*. Minnetonka, MN: Creative Publishing international, 2005.

Lewis, Gary. *Complete Guide to Hunting: Basic Techniques for Gun & Bow Hunters*. Minnetonka, MN: Creative Publishing International, 2008.

Smith, Jason. *Dog Training: Retrievers and Pointing Dogs*. Minnetonka, MN: Creative Publishing international, 2007.

Tarrant, Bill. *How to Hunt Birds with Gun Dogs*. Harrisburg, PA: Stackpole Books, 2003.

BIBLIOGRAPHY

Baird, Joel Banner. "Hunters as Environmental Stewards." November 29, 2009. Retrieved January 2, 2010 (http://www.burlingtonfreepress.com/article/20091129/LIVING09/91125050/Hunters-as-environmental-stewards).

Baker, Scott. "Squirrel Hunting: The Basics of the Techniques." August 15, 2008. Retrieved February 5, 2010 (http://www.associatedcontent.com/article/50414/squirrel_hunting_the_basics_of_the.html?cat=11).

Boddington, Craig. *Fair Chase in North America*. Missoula, MT: Boone & Crockett Club, 2004.

Brakefield, Tom. *Small Game Hunting*. Philadelphia, PA: J. B. Lippincott Company, 1978.

Dressing and Cooking Wild Game. Chanhassen, MN: Creative Publishing, 2000.

Ellman, Robert. *The Game Bird Hunter's Bible*. New York, NY, Doubleday, 1993.

Geer, Galen. *Meat on the Table: Modern Small-Game Hunting*. Boulder, CO: Paladin Press, 1985.

Gunners, Den. "Small Game Hunting." 2007. Retrieved February 8, 2010 (http://www.gunnersden.com/index.htm.hunting-small-game.html).

Harrington, Dan. (Avid Woodcock Hunter, Spooner, WI) in discussion with the author, February 2010.

Hehner, Mike, Chris Dorsey, and Greg Breining. *North American Game Birds*. Minnetonka, MN: Cy Decosse, 1996.

Lawrence, H. Lea. *The Ultimate Guide to Small Game and Varmint Hunting: How to Hunt Squirrels, Rabbits, Hares, Woodchucks, Coyotes, Foxes and More*. Guilford, CT: Lyons Press, 2002.

Lemke, Chris. (Outdoor Connection, Two Harbors, MN) in discussion with the author, February 2010.

Maas, David R. *North American Game Animals*. Minnetonka, MN: Cy Decosse, 1995.

Meili, Launi. *Rifle: Steps to Success*. Champaign, IL: Human Kinetics, 2008.

Michigan Natural Resources and Environment. "Hunting Small Game Helps Kids Become Good Hunters." January 20, 2006. Retrieved February 2, 2010 (http://www.michigan.gov/dnr/0,1607,7-153-10366_46403_46404-135534--,00.html).

Minnesota Firearms Safety Hunter Education, Student Manual. Seattle, WA: Outdoor Empire Publishing, 2001.

Motes, J. "Techniques and Tips for Rabbit Hunting Without a Dog." December 7, 2007. Retrieved February 7, 2010 (http://www.associated-content.com/article/466426/techniques_and_tips_for_rabbit_hunting.html?cat=11).

National Shooting Sports Foundation. "The Ethical Hunter." Pamphlet, 2006.

National Shooting Sports Foundation. "Firearms Safety Depends on You." Pamphlet, 2006.

National Shooting Sports Foundation. "The Hunter and Conservation." Booklet, 2006.

Peterson, David H. (Hunter Education Instructor, Two Harbors, MN) in discussion with the author, February 2010.

Schneck, Marcus. *The North America Hunter's Handbook*. Philadelphia, PA: Running Press, 1991.

Smith, Richard P. *Hunting Rabbits & Hares: The Complete Guide to North America's Favorite Small Game*. Harrisburg, PA: Stackpole Books, 1986.

Sternberg, Dick. *Upland Game Birds*. Minnetonka, MN: Cy Decosse, 1995.

Tarrant, Bill. *The Field & Stream Upland Bird Hunting Handbook*. Guilford, CT: Lyons Press, 1999.

U.S. Fish and Wildlife Service. "Migratory Bird Harvest Information Program (HIP)" September 9, 2009. Retrieved February 7, 2010 (http://www.fws.gov/hip).

Index

About the Author

Judy Monroe Peterson is married to an avid hunter who has more than fifty years of hunting experience. She has earned two master's degrees and is the author of more than fifty educational books for young people. Currently, she is a writer and editor of K–12 and post–high school curriculum materials on a variety of subjects, including biology, life science, and the environment.

About the Consultant

Benjamin Cowan has more than twenty years of both big game and small game hunting experience. In addition to being an avid hunter, Cowan is also a member of many conservation organizations. He currently resides in west Tennessee.

Photo Credits

Cover, pp. 1, 3 © www.istockphoto.com/Stephen Kane; p. 5 Don Farrall/Photodisc/Getty Images; pp. 7, 16, 25, 36, 44 (silhouettes) © www.istockphoto.com/Michael Olson and Hemera/Thinkstock; pp. 8, 11, 14, 28, 30, 37, 45 Shutterstock.com; p. 13 Nicole Russo; p. 17 Minnesota Department of Natural Resources; pp. 18–19 © www.istockphoto.com/Andrew Hyslop; p. 22 Julieann Wallace; p. 26 Jupiterimages/Comstock Images/Getty Images; p. 27 © www.istockphoto.com/Paul Tessier; p. 33 © www.istockphoto.com/Steven Myers; p. 34 Richard Baetsen/U.S. Fish & Wildlife Service; p. 41 Joel Sartore/National Geographic Image Collection/Getty Images; p. 43 © www.istockphoto.com/Daniel Mar; p. 47 Hannah Stouffer/Getty Images; p. 48 © www.istockphoto.com/Matt Stauss; p. 52 U.S. Fish & Wildlife Service; back cover (silhouette) Hemera/Thinkstock.

Designer: Nicole Russo; Editor: Kathy Kuhtz Campbell;
Photo Researcher: Peter Tomlinson